Flavored Butter Recipes

MAKE YOUR BUTTER EVEN BETTER

NATALIE OLIVER

Table of Contents

A Note From Natalie 1

About Flavored Butters 3
    What is a compound butter? 3
    Why use a flavored butter? 3
    How to use compound butters 3
    How to store compound butter 4

General Preparation Method 7

Flavored Butter Recipes 9
    Savory 11
        Classic Maitre d'Hotel Butter 11
        Roasted Red Pepper Butter 11
        Basil Butter 12
        Rosemary Mint Butter 12
        Chipotle Lime Butter 13
        Red Wine Butter 13
        Bacon Butter 14
        Sun Dried Tomato Basil Butter 14
        Spicy Curry Butter 15
        Avocado Lime Butter 15
        Honey Worcestershire Butter 16
        Moroccan Spice Butter 17
        Garlic Chile Butter 18
        Caper Butter 18
        Dijon Chive Butter 19
        Herb Butter 19
        Roasted Garlic Butter 20
        Orange Roasted Jalapeno Butter 21

Cheddar Butter 21

Blue Cheese Butter 22

Smokey Chili Butter 22

Sweet 23

Cinnamon Honey Butter 23

Maple Orange Butter 23

Salted Caramel Butter 24

Honey Peach Butter 25

Rum Raisin Butter 25

Ginger Pecan Butter 26

Cranberry Orange Butter 26

Cherry Amaretto Butter 27

Strawberry Mint Butter 27

Citrus and Sage Butter 28

Mojito Butter 29

Recipes Using Flavored Butter 31

Main Dishes 33

Grilled Chicken Breast with Basil Butter 33

Lamb Chops with Rosemary Mint Butter 35

Pork Medallions with Chipotle Lime Butter 36

New York Strip Beef Steak with Red Wine Butter 37

Baked Oysters in Garlic Chili Butter 38

Shrimp Fettuccine 39

Oven Roasted Salmon with Orange Jalapeno Butter 40

Chicken Wings with Blue Cheese Butter 41

Pork Chops with Cherry Pan Sauce 42

Side Dishes 43
Chipotle Carrots 43
Pan Fried Potatoes with Bacon Butter 44
Roasted Asparagus with Prosciutto and Sun Dried Tomato Basil Butter 45
Moroccan Mashed Sweet Potatoes 46
Roasted Corn on the Cob with Smokey Chili Butter 47
Roasted Butternut Squash with Citrus Sage Butter 48
Pepper and Onion Saute 49

Sandwiches 51
Cajun Roast Beef Sandwich 51
California Smoked Turkey Sandwich 52
Ham and Cheese Sliders 53
Huge Pub Style White Cheddar Burgers 54

Recipe Books from Natalie 59
One Last Thing 60
Notes 61

A Note From Natalie

Butter sometimes gets pushed aside for healthier options. To be honest, it's probably not the best health decision to load every dish down with butter. Butter in moderation, however, is a very good thing. It adds flavor and richness to any recipe. For me, a baguette with soft, creamy butter is almost Heaven.

Butter by itself is good. Great, even. Add a few ingredients to create a decadent condiment or a flavor enhancement for your favorite dish and you've got a winner.

Making a flavored butter isn't a complicated process at all. Anyone can do it. I've put together some of my favorite and most used recipes for compound butter. I've also included some recipes for ways you can use them.

So, get ready to explore the brave new world of butter indulgence!

Want to find out when I publish a new book or when I have a sale? Sign up here and you'll always be in the loop!

http://recipesfromeverywhere.com/SignUp

P.S. You'll even get a tasty little bonus!

About Flavored Butters

WHAT IS A COMPOUND BUTTER?
You might not be clear on what flavored butters really are. It's simple. It's butter with other stuff mixed into it. In the culinary world, these butters are referred to as compound butter because they have butter with other components added. A compound butter is also called a flavored butter.

WHY USE A FLAVORED BUTTER?
Compound butters add flavor, color, interest, and depth to the recipes they're used in. While they do make a beautiful presentation when presented on top of a perfectly grilled steak or piece of salmon, they add remarkable flavor. This is the real reason I'm a big fan of compound butters.

HOW TO USE COMPOUND BUTTERS
You can spread compound butter on bread or top meat or fish with it. One of the easiest and most common ways to use a flavored butter is to place a dollop or slice on top of a steak right as it's about to be served. The butter will melt into the meat and the herbs or flavors will blend to make a delicious sauce. Restaurants use this method all the time with great success. It's very easy to do it at home. If you want your home cooked meal to have some of the elements of a restaurant entrée, finish it with some compound butter.

Add compound butter to sauces and gravies when butter is called for to add richness. Have you ever made a pan gravy or sauce that called for butter to be added at the end of the cooking time? You can whisk in a flavored butter for that if you have some available. Or, make a butter that fits with the profile of the meal, use it in the pan sauce, and then serve it with the bread. Using the same flavor profile in more than one place creates a cohesive component to your meal and makes it all "work" to be memorable.

Sweet compound butters are great with croissants, pancakes, waffles, and muffins for breakfast or brunch. These can also replace plain butter in frostings and fillings. Depending on the ingredients in a sweet butter, it could very easily be the perfect topping for fish or meat. If you pair a sweet component, such as some sort of fruit, with an herb, you end up with a flavored butter that is perfect for a savory dish.

Use a flavored butter in recipes when butter is called for when the flavor profile makes sense. If you're making a dish that calls for butter, use a flavored butter instead of plain butter. For example, if you like to finish steamed vegetables with butter, use flavored butter. If you're making a seafood pasta dish that includes some butter, use a herb butter to punch it up.

Any time you use a flavored butter in a recipe, though, make sure that the butter you use matches the profile of the recipe or the meal. For example, you may not want to use a thyme and sage butter on a dish that already has basil and sun dried tomatoes in it. That would probably create a competing flavor set that would just cause all the flavors to get muddy and confused. So just make sure to use a flavored butter that makes sense with the rest of the flavors in your meal. The flavors should always complement each other, not compete.

To expand just a little about complementing flavors, be sure to know who you're cooking for. If you know your family likes a certain combination of flavors that may be a little outside the typical profile, go for it. Just because a famous chef says something shouldn't be served together, doesn't make it always true. Cook what you like and serve the food your family loves. That's one of the most important rules of cooking for me.

HOW TO STORE COMPOUND BUTTER

Most of my research tells me that a compound butter will last up to about a week wrapped well in the refrigerator. I think that in some cases compound butter will keep longer in the refrigerator if it's wrapped well. If your butter contains garlic, it may be best to freeze it if you won't use it in about a week. The garlic can start to taste a little off after a few days. Butters that contain only herbs will last much longer in the fridge. Just be sure to wrap your compound butter really well to preserve the flavor and not allow the butter to absorb other flavors.

You can freeze compound butter for about four to five months. One of the best ways to do this is to slice the butter into portions before you wrap it for the freezer. This will make it easier to use it by allowing you to take only the amount you want and not have to defrost the whole portion if you don't need it all. To wrap your butter for the freezer, double wrap it in plastic wrap and place that in a zip lock freezer bag. Be sure to date your package so you'll know how long it's been there.

If you've made butter that is looser and is meant to be more spreadable, you can store this butter in the fridge in a plastic container with a tight lid. If you want to freeze it, I've found that if you transfer the butter to a zip lock freezer bag, you can spread the mixture out into a flat disk about a quarter to a half inch thick. This will allow you to break off the amount you need without having to thaw the whole amount out if you don't need it all. If you do need it all, it will thaw much quicker than if it was in a thick block.

General Preparation Method

All compound butters are created in the same general method. There may be a few variations for the ingredients, which we'll review later, but all in all everything is always done the same way.

I prefer to always use unsalted butter. This will allow you to season the butter as you wish. It's important to remember, however, if you do use unsalted butter you must add salt back in. Leaving out the salt will make your butter bland and the rest of the ingredients will seem flat. Even if you're preparing a sweet butter, salt is still needed. Adding salt to sweet things enhances the sweetness of the ingredients. Adding salt will help add balance and keep the butter from tasting bland.

Bring the butter to room temperature in it's original packaging. A stick of butter should sit on the counter top in it's paper wrapping on a plate until it's soft. Do not use the microwave to soften it. Do not let it melt. If you're in a hurry, you can take the butter out of the packaging and cut it into small pieces. That will help it soften quicker. I still think it's important to not use the microwave because the softening will not be even and you can't control how it goes.

Chop any herbs or ingredients finely. Big chunks of ingredients in the butter make it more difficult to slice evenly. You may be looking for a rustic look and that's okay, but it's still better to have the butter easy to slice. Most importantly, big chunks of ingredients in the butter can make it have an unbalanced flavor. It would be easy to cut the butter into slices that are heavy on one flavor and light on another if your ingredients are chopped too largely or unevenly. Your goal is that every slice of butter has the perfect balance of flavor.

If you're adding ingredients that need to be cooked first, be sure you allow enough time for those items to cook and then cool to room temperature. Adding hot or even warm ingredients to the butter will melt it. Once the butter is melted, you won't be able to get it back to the consistency you need to roll it and slice it or to pipe it into shapes.

You can use a food processor, blender, mixer, or a fork to mix your softened butter with the added ingredients. I most often just use a fork. It's easy to place everything into a mixing bowl and mix it all together

General Preparation Method

with a fork. This makes clean up much faster. It's not a bad thing to get out an appliance you like to use, but this blending process takes such a short time that I prefer to not hassle with getting out the food processor and then cleaning it up to put it away when I'm done – 45 seconds later. This is totally up to you and any method you choose is fine. If you need to have a whipped butter, however, I recommend using a hand mixer.

Once your butter is mixed, spoon it out onto a piece of parchment paper and shape it into a log. Wrap the log in plastic wrap and chill it until firm and then slice it.

Another option is to place the butter into a pastry bag and pipe rosettes onto parchment lined baking sheet. Chill until the rosettes are firm. You can then place the rosettes of butter into a zip lock bag or a plastic container with a cover.

There are some butters that are a little looser in texture – most of the time these have more liquid ingredients added. These will be more difficult to shape into a solid form so it's best to put these in bowls and serve at room temperature or at least close. These will be more spreadable this way.

Any compound butter can be served as a spread – just like plain butter can. If you want to serve the butter as a spread for bread or crackers, place the butter in your serving dish. You can chill it and set it out early enough for it to come back to room temperature in time for serving so that it's spreadable.

Flavored Butter Recipes

When making a compound butter, feel free to adjust the drier ingredients as you prefer – up or down. Herbs and chopped vegetables are easily incorporated into the butter and a little more or less to meet your taste will not affect the way the final product comes together.

If the recipe calls for liquid or wet ingredients such as fruit juices, honey, or jam it's wise to adjust with a little caution. Adding more liquid to the butter could make it more difficult for the butter to chill into a solid block. While this isn't a big issue, it's just something you may want to be aware of. If you're simply using the butter as a spread at room temperature (or close) this won't matter at all.

Flavored butters are a great place to experiment, so change things up and make your butter the way you like it. I suggest coming up with your own signature flavored butter and use it every chance you get!

SAVORY

Classic Maitre d'Hotel Butter

Ingredients

1/4 lb unsalted butter, softened to room temperature
2 TBSP flat leaf parsley, chopped
2 tsp lemon juice
1 tsp salt
1/2 tsp white pepper

Directions

Mix all ingredients together. Shape the butter, wrap in plastic wrap, chill.

Roasted Red Pepper Butter

Ingredients

1/4 lb unsalted butter, softened to room temperature
2 oz roasted red pepper, pureed
1 tsp lemon juice
1 tsp salt

Directions

Mix all ingredients together. Shape the butter, wrap in plastic wrap, chill.

Basil Butter

Ingredients

1/4 lb unsalted butter, softened to room temperature
2 TBSP basil, chopped
1 small shallot, minced
1 tsp lemon juice
1 tsp salt

Directions

Mix all ingredients together. Shape the butter, wrap in plastic wrap, chill.

Rosemary Mint Butter

Ingredients

1/4 lb unsalted butter, softened to room temperature
2 TBSP mint, chopped
1 TBSP rosemary, chopped
2 tsp brown sugar
1 tsp salt
1 tsp cracked black pepper

Directions

Mix all ingredients together. Shape the butter, wrap in plastic wrap, chill.

Chipotle Lime Butter

Ingredients

1/4 lb unsalted butter, softened to room temperature
2 chipotle peppers, from can in adobo sauce, minced
2 tsp lime juice
1 tsp salt
1 tsp ground coriander
1/2 tsp ground cumin

Directions

Mix all ingredients together. Shape the butter, wrap in plastic wrap, chill.

Red Wine Butter

Ingredients

1/4 lb unsalted butter, softened to room temperature
1 tsp salt
1 cup red wine
1 large sprig rosemary

Directions

Place wine in a saucepan with the rosemary sprig. Bring to a boil over high heat. Reduce heat to medium and continue to cook. Reduce the wine until it's syrupy. Discard the rosemary sprig. Set aside to cool to room temperature.

Mix the red wine syrup with the room temperature butter and the salt. Shape the butter, wrap in plastic wrap, chill.

BACON BUTTER

Ingredients

1/4 lb unsalted butter, softened to room temperature
1 tsp salt
1 tsp cracked black pepper
1 TBSP red wine vinegar
6 strips bacon
2 shallots, chopped

Directions

Chop the bacon. Saute the bacon with the shallots until bacon is crispy and shallots are soft. Drain on paper towels. Cool to room temperature.

Mix the cooled bacon and shallot mixture with the room temperature butter, salt, pepper, and vinegar. Shape the butter, wrap in plastic wrap, chill.

SUN DRIED TOMATO BASIL BUTTER

Ingredients

1/4 lb unsalted butter, softened to room temperature
6 sun dried tomatoes, packed in olive oil, minced
2 TBSP basil, chopped
1 tsp salt
1/2 tsp cracked pepper
1 tsp red wine vinegar

Directions

Mix all ingredients together. Shape the butter, wrap in plastic wrap, chill.

Spicy Curry Butter

Ingredients

1/4 lb unsalted butter, softened to room temperature
1 TBSP curry powder
1 TBSP ground coriander
1 tsp salt
1 tsp turmeric
1 TBSP honey
1/2 tsp red pepper flakes

Directions

Mix all ingredients together. Shape the butter, wrap in plastic wrap, chill.

Avocado Lime Butter

Ingredients

1/4 lb unsalted butter, softened to room temperature
1 tsp salt
1 avocado, mashed
Juice from one lime
Zest from one lime, grated

Directions

Mix all ingredients together. Shape the butter, wrap in plastic wrap, chill.

Honey Worcestershire Butter

Ingredients

1/4 lb unsalted butter, softened to room temperature
1/2 tsp salt
1 tsp cracked pepper
3 TBSP honey
3 TBSP Worcestershire sauce
1 green onion, finely diced

Directions

Mix all ingredients together. This butter will be better if placed in a storage container and covered for storage. This butter does not get as firm as most other butters.

SAVORY

Moroccan Spice Butter

Ingredients

1/4 lb unsalted butter, softened to room temperature
1 tsp salt
1 tsp cumin, ground
1 tsp garlic, minced
1 TBSP ginger, grated
1 TBSP olive oil
1/2 tsp turmeric
1/2 tsp ground cumin
1/2 tsp ground coriander
1/2 tsp cinnamon
1/4 tsp red pepper flakes
1 tsp lemon zest, grated
4 TBSP cilantro, chopped

Directions

Heat the olive oil over medium heat and lightly saute the garlic and ginger. Cool to room temperature.

Mix all ingredients together when the garlic and ginger mixture is cool. Shape the butter, wrap in plastic wrap, and chill.

GARLIC CHILE BUTTER

Ingredients

1/4 lb unsalted butter, softened to room temperature
1 tsp salt
2 cloves garlic, minced
1 TBSP Sriracha
1 tsp red pepper flakes
1 tsp lemon zest, grated
1 TBSP lemon juice
Dash of Ancho chili powder

Directions

Mix all ingredients together. Shape the butter, wrap in plastic wrap, and chill.

CAPER BUTTER

Ingredients

1/4 lb unsalted butter, softened to room temperature
1 tsp salt
1 clove garlic, minced
2 TBSP capers, chopped
1 tsp lemon zest, grated
1 tsp red wine vinegar
2 TBSP parsley, chopped
Pinch of cayenne

Directions

Mix all ingredients together. Shape the butter, wrap in plastic wrap, and chill.

Dijon Chive Butter

Ingredients

1/4 lb unsalted butter, softened to room temperature
1 tsp salt
1 clove garlic, minced
2 TBSP chives, chopped
1 TBSP parsley, chopped
2 TBSP Dijon mustard
2 tsp Worcestershire sauce

Directions

Mix all ingredients together. Shape the butter, wrap in plastic wrap, and chill.

Herb Butter

Ingredients

1/4 lb unsalted butter, softened to room temperature
1 tsp salt
1 clove garlic, minced
1 TBSP oregano, chopped
1 TBSP parsley, chopped
1 TBSP rosemary, chopped
1 TBSP thyme, chopped

Directions

Mix all ingredients together. Shape the butter, wrap in plastic wrap, and chill.

Roasted Garlic Butter

Ingredients

1 head garlic
1 TBSP olive oil
1/4 lb unsalted butter, softened to room temperature
2 tsp salt
1 tsp pepper

Directions

Heat the oven to 350F.

Cut the top of the head of garlic off, leaving the cloves attached at the root. Remove the loose outside skins. Place the garlic bulb in foil, root side down. Drizzle with the olive oil. Roast in the oven for 30 to 45 minutes, until the garlic is soft and lightly browned. Remove from the oven and cool.

When the garlic is cool enough to easily handle, gently squeeze the roasted garlic pulp into a bowl. Cool to room temperature.

Mash the cooled garlic with the salt and pepper. Add the room temperature butter and mix it together well.

Shape the butter, wrap it in plastic wrap and chill.

Orange Roasted Jalapeno Butter

Ingredients

1/4 lb unsalted butter, softened to room temperature
2 tsp salt
1 large jalapeno
1 TBSP fresh orange juice
1 TBSP orange zest, grated

Directions

Heat oven to 375F.

Cut the top off of the pepper, cut in half lengthwise, and remove the seeds and membrane. Place on a small sheet pan and roast in the oven until soft. Remove from the oven and cool to room temperature.

Chop the roasted jalapeno finely. Mix it with the remaining ingredients. Shape the butter, wrap in plastic wrap, and chill.

Cheddar Butter

Ingredients

1/4 lb unsalted butter, softened to room temperature
2 tsp salt
1/2 cup cheddar, finely grated
1/2 tsp cayenne
1 tsp Worcestershire sauce

Directions

Mix all ingredients together. Shape the butter, wrap in plastic wrap, and chill.

Blue Cheese Butter

Ingredients

1/4 lb unsalted butter, softened to room temperature
2 tsp salt
1/2 cup blue cheese, crumbled
2 TBSP parsley, chopped
1/2 tsp cayenne
1 tsp Worcestershire sauce
2 TBSP brandy
1 clove garlic, minced

Directions

Mix all ingredients together. Shape the butter, wrap in plastic wrap, and chill.

Smokey Chili Butter

Ingredients

1/4 lb unsalted butter, softened to room temperature
1 tsp salt
1/2 tsp cracked pepper
1 tsp Worcestershire sauce
1/2 tsp Tobasco
1 tsp cumin
1 tsp smoked paprika
1/2 tsp garlic powder
1 TBSP oregano

Directions

Mix all ingredients together. Shape the butter, wrap in plastic wrap, chill.

S‌WEET

C‌INNAMON H‌ONEY B‌UTTER

Ingredients

1/4 lb unsalted butter, softened to room temperature
1/2 tsp salt
1 tsp ground cinnamon
1 tsp vanilla extract
1/3 cup honey

Directions

Mix all ingredients together. Shape the butter, wrap in plastic wrap, chill.

M‌APLE O‌RANGE B‌UTTER

Ingredients

1/4 lb unsalted butter, softened to room temperature
1/2 tsp salt
2 TBSP maple syrup
1 tsp vanilla extract
2 TBSP fresh orange juice
2 tsp orange zest, grated

Directions

Mix all ingredients together. Shape the butter, wrap in plastic wrap, chill.

Salted Caramel Butter

Ingredients

1/4 lb unsalted butter, softened to room temperature
1/4 cup white sugar
3 TBSP water
1/4 cup heavy cream
1/2 tsp coarse sea salt
1/4 tsp vanilla extract

Directions

Place the sugar and water in a heavy saucepan. Bring the mixture to a boil and brush down the sides of the saucepan with water. Boil for approximately six minutes. As the sugar mixture starts to color, begin swirling it in the pan to ensure it cooks evenly.

When the sugar mixture reaches a caramel amber color, remove it from the heat. Very slowly, add the cream. It will splatter in the hot liquid. Stir the mixture very well. Set aside to cool.

Blend the cooled caramel with the butter, salt, and vanilla. Shape, wrap with plastic wrap, and chill.

If you prefer, you can leave the salted caramel butter at room temperature and use it as a buttercream frosting for cupcakes or cookies.

Honey Peach Butter

Ingredients

1/4 lb unsalted butter, softened to room temperature
1/2 tsp salt
8 TBSP honey
1 tsp vanilla extract
1/2 cup fresh peaches, mashed

Directions

Mix all ingredients together using an electric mixer. Because of the high honey content, beat for 8 to 10 minutes to get the butter light and fluffy.

Place in a storage bowl and press plastic wrap on top of the butter. Chill.

Rum Raisin Butter

Ingredients

1/4 lb unsalted butter, softened to room temperature
1/2 tsp salt
4 TBSP raisins, chopped
1/2 tsp vanilla extract
2 TBSP dark rum
2 TBSP brown sugar

Directions

Mix all ingredients together. Shape the butter, wrap in plastic wrap, and chill.

GINGER PECAN BUTTER

Ingredients

1/4 lb unsalted butter, softened to room temperature
1/2 tsp salt
2 TBSP crystallized ginger, finely chopped
1/3 cup pecans, finely chopped
1/2 tsp vanilla extract
2 TBSP brown sugar

Directions

Mix all ingredients together. Shape the butter, wrap in plastic wrap, and chill.

CRANBERRY ORANGE BUTTER

Ingredients

1/4 lb unsalted butter, softened to room temperature
1/2 tsp salt
4 TBSP dried cranberries, finely chopped
8 TBSP fresh orange juice
1 TBSP orange zest
2 TBSP honey

Directions

Combine the salt, cranberries, orange juice, orange zest, and honey in a small saucepan. Bring to a boil over medium high heat. Boil until the liquid is reduced by half.

Remove from the heat and cool to room temperature.

Mix the cooled cranberry mixture with the butter. Shape the butter, wrap it in plastic wrap, and chill.

CHERRY AMARETTO BUTTER

Ingredients

1/4 lb unsalted butter, softened to room temperature
1/2 tsp salt
4 TBSP cherry preserves, mashed
2 TBSP Amaretto liqueur

Directions

Mix all ingredients together. Shape the butter, wrap in plastic wrap, and chill.

STRAWBERRY MINT BUTTER

Ingredients

1/4 lb unsalted butter, softened to room temperature
1/2 tsp salt
4 TBSP strawberry preserves, mashed
1 TBSP mint, finely chopped

Directions

Mix all ingredients together. Shape the butter, wrap in plastic wrap, and chill.

CITRUS AND SAGE BUTTER

Ingredients

1/4 lb unsalted butter, softened to room temperature
1/2 tsp salt
1 TBSP orange juice
1 TBSP lemon juice
1 TBSP lime juice
2 tsp orange zest
2 tsp lemon zest
2 tsp lime zest
2 tsp sage, finely chopped
1 TBSP parsley, finely chopped
Pinch red pepper flakes

Directions

Mix all ingredients together. Shape the butter, wrap in plastic wrap, and chill.

Mojito Butter

Ingredients

1/4 lb unsalted butter, softened to room temperature
1/2 tsp salt
2 TBSP light rum
2 TBSP lime juice
1 TBSP lime zest
1 TBSP honey
2 TBSP mint, finely chopped

Directions

Mix all ingredients together. Shape the butter, wrap in plastic wrap, and chill.

Recipes Using Flavored Butter

The recipes you'll find here are recipes that call for compound butter. The recipes for the compound butter needed in each recipe can be found in the Flavored Butter Recipes section. You will make the compound butter to go with the recipe you're making for dinner.

Use any leftover butter to spread on bread or flavor another recipe later. Follow the freezing recommendation at the start of this book in the Storage section if you won't be using all of the butter at that time.

Each recipe serves 4 people.

Main Dishes

Grilled Chicken Breast with Basil Butter

Ingredients

4 chicken breasts, with bone and skin
8 whole basil leaves
1 TBSP garlic, minced
1/4 cup onion, diced
2 cups white wine
1/2 cup white wine vinegar
2 bay leaves
2 TBSP thyme, chopped
1 tsp pepper
1 TBSP salt
2 TBSP lemon juice
1/2 cup olive oil
Basil Butter

Directions

Mix the garlic, onion, white wine, vinegar, bay leaves, thyme, pepper, salt, lemon juice, and olive oil. Pour into a large zip lock bag. Set aside.

Carefully pull the skin away from the meat on the chicken breast. Place two basil leaves under the skin to cover the meat on each breast.

Place the chicken breast pieces in the marinade inside the zip lock bag. Marinate for one to two hours in the refrigerator.

Heat the grill. Remove the chicken from the marinade and pat dry. Discard the marinade.

Melt about a third of the basil butter and place in a small bowl. Brush the chicken with the basil butter and place it on the grill skin side down. Turn the chicken once or twice only basting with the basil butter periodically.

Serve the chicken with a slice or two of the basil butter melting over each piece.

Lamb Chops with Rosemary Mint Butter

Ingredients

8 small lamb chops
Salt and pepper
Olive oil
Rosemary Mint Butter

Directions

Preheat the grill.

Brush each chop with oil and season with salt and pepper.

Grill each lamb chop to the desired temperature making cross hatched grill marks on each one.

Place two chops on each plate or place all of them down the center of a large serving platter. While the chops are still hot, top each one with a liberal slice of rosemary mint butter. If the butter needs help melting, place the platter or plates briefly under a broiler to help melt the butter.

Pork Medallions with Chipotle Lime Butter

Ingredients

2 pork tenderloins, trimmed and sliced into one inch thick medallions
1 TBSP salt
2 tsp ground Chipotle pepper
2 tsp ground coriander
Olive oil
4 TBSP honey
1/3 cup apple cider
2 TBSP cider vinegar
Chipotle Lime Butter
2 green onions, sliced

Directions

Mix the salt, Chipotle pepper, and coriander in a small bowl. Season the pork pieces with the Chipotle mixture on all sides.

Heat the olive oil in a large skillet over medium high heat. Add the pork and sear until lightly browned, about two minutes. Turn the pork and sear on the other side for about two minutes.

Remove the pork from the pan and cover with foil.

Add the honey, cider, and vinegar to the pan. Mix together and bring to a boil. Reduce heat to medium and return the pork medallions to the pan. Turn to coat each piece in the sauce. Continue to cook for another four to five minutes.

Remove the pork medallions and place them on a serving platter. Set aside.

Add the Chipotle Lime Butter to the cider sauce in the pan. Stir until butter is melted. Drizzle butter sauce over the pork on the serving platter. Garnish with the sliced green onions.

New York Strip Beef Steak with Red Wine Butter

Ingredients

4 cloves garlic, chopped
2 TBSP rosemary, chopped
1 TBSP salt
3 TBSP olive oil
4 New York strip steaks
Red Wine Butter, at room temperature

Directions

Mix the garlic, rosemary, salt, and olive oil together. Rub into both sides of each steak. Let stand 20 minutes at room temperature.

Heat the grill.

Grill the steaks to desired temperature. Let rest at least 10 minutes.

Serve steaks smeared with the red wine butter.

Baked Oysters in Garlic Chili Butter

Ingredients

2-3 lbs fresh oysters
Garlic Chili Butter
Juice of one lemon
2 TBSP flat leaf parsley, chopped

Directions

Heat oven to 450F.

Place a thick layer of coarse salt on a large baking sheet. Shuck the oysters retaining as much of the juices as possible. Discard the top shell.

Place each oyster in the bottom half of its shell into the salt. Top each oyster with a slice of the Garlic Chile Butter.

Bake until oysters start to curl around the edges, about 10 to 12 minutes.

Sprinkle with the lemon juice and parsley.

Shrimp Fettuccine

Ingredients

2 lbs shrimp, shelled and deveined
2 TBSP olive oil
2 large tomatoes, chopped
4 oz Herb Butter
1 lb fettuccine, cooked
Salt
Pepper
Juice from one lemon

Directions

Cook pasta according to package directions.

While pasta cooks, heat the olive oil in a large skillet over medium high heat. Saute the shrimp in the hot oil until pink. Remove from the skillet to a plate. Set aside.

Add the Herb Butter to the skillet and melt over medium heat. Add the chopped tomatoes and cook to warm the tomatoes through and start to break them down slightly.

Drain the pasta and add it to the skillet with the butter and tomatoes. Add the shrimp and toss together.

Oven Roasted Salmon with Orange Jalapeno Butter

Ingredients

4 salmon filets
Salt and pepper
Olive oil
4 TBSP fresh orange juice
Orange Jalapeno Butter
1 TBSP green onions, sliced

Directions

Heat the oven to 400F.

Brush each salmon filet with olive oil. Season with salt and pepper. Place on a sheet pan and pour the orange juice over the fish.

Roast for 8 to 10 minutes for a 1 inch thick piece of fish. Roast longer for thicker pieces.

When the fish is done, place on a serving platter and top each filet with a liberal slice of the Orange Jalapeno Butter. Sprinkle with the sliced green onions.

CHICKEN WINGS WITH BLUE CHEESE BUTTER

Ingredients

2 lbs chicken wings, tips removed and joints separated
1 cup bottled Buffalo wing sauce
1 cup celery, chopped
1/4 cup green onion, chopped
6 oz Blue Cheese Butter

Directions

Heat oven to 400F.

Place wings on a large parchment paper lined sheet pan. Bake for 30 to 40 minutes until chicken skin is crispy and chicken is done. Turn wings over halfway through cooking.

Place cooked wings in a large mixing bowl with the celery and green onions. Toss with the Buffalo sauce. Add the Blue Cheese Butter and toss again to melt the butter.

Place on a serving platter.

Pork Chops with Cherry Pan Sauce

Ingredients

4 pork chops, bone in
Salt and pepper
1 TBSP olive oil
2 cups red wine vinegar
1/4 cup beef stock
1/3 cup chicken stock
1/3 cup brown sugar
3 TBSP cherry preserves
3/4 cup dried cherries
3 TBSP Cherry Amaretto Butter

Directions

Combine the vinegar, stocks, sugar, and preserves in a heavy sauce pan. Bring to a boil over high heat. Reduce to medium and simmer to reduce volume by half. Add the dried cherries and remove from the heat. Set aside.

Heat the grill to high heat. Brush each pork chop lightly with olive oil on each side and season liberally with salt and pepper. Grill the chops to an internal temperature of 145F.

Cover the chops with foil to keep warm.

Heat the cherry sauce over medium high heat. When it's almost to the boiling point, whisk in the Cherry Amaretto Butter.

Serve the chops with the cherry pan sauce.

SIDE DISHES

CHIPOTLE CARROTS

Ingredients

1 lb carrots, peeled and chopped
1/4 cup red bell pepper, diced
1 TBSP olive oil
4 TBSP Chipotle Lime Butter
2 TBSP cilantro, chopped

Directions

Boil carrots in generously salted water until slightly tender but not completely done. Remove from heat and drain.

Heat olive oil in skillet. Add drained carrots and red bell pepper. Saute until carrots are done and red bell pepper is softened. Continue to saute until carrots start to get a little bit of a crispy outside.

Add the Chipotle Lime Butter and continue to cook until butter is melted and coats the vegetables. Remove from heat and place in a serving bowl. Garnish with chopped cilantro.

PAN FRIED POTATOES WITH BACON BUTTER

Ingredients

3 Idaho potatoes, peeled and chopped
1 TBSP olive oil
6 TBSP Bacon Butter
2 TBSP flat leaf parsley, chopped
4 TBSP baby arugula, chopped
1 TBSP chives, chopped

Directions

Boil potatoes in generously salted water until slightly tender but not completely done. Remove from heat and drain.

Add olive oil and bacon butter to a skillet and heat over medium heat to melt butter. Add potatoes. Cook potatoes, turning frequently, until crispy and completely tender.

Top with parsley, arugula, and chives.

Roasted Asparagus with Prosciutto and Sun Dried Tomato Basil Butter

Ingredients

1 lb asparagus, trimmed
2 oz Prosciutto, chopped
2 shallots, chopped
2 TBSP olive oil
2 TBSP Sun Dried Tomato Basil Butter

Directions

Heat the oven to 400F.

Drizzle the asparagus with half of the olive oil and season with salt and pepper. Roast until the asparagus is tender.

In a skillet, heat the remaining olive oil. Saute the Prosciutto and shallots until the Prosciutto is slightly crispy and the shallots are soft. Add the Sun Dried Tomato Basil Butter and continue cooking over medium heat until the butter is melted. Give a final stir to combine melted butter with the Prosciutto and shallot mixture.

Place the roasted asparagus on a serving platter and top with the Prosciutto mixture.

MOROCCAN MASHED SWEET POTATOES

Ingredients

2 large sweet potatoes
4 TBSP heavy cream
Salt and pepper to taste
4 TBSP Moroccan Spice Butter, melted

Directions

Heat the oven to 350F. Wrap each sweet potato in foil and place on a baking sheet.

Bake until the potatoes are completely tender. This will take around two hours.

When the potatoes are cool enough to handle, peel them and discard the skins.

Mash the potatoes with a potato masher until they're broken up and starting to break down. Add the cream and the melted butter. Continue to mash until the potatoes are completely mashed. Mix with a spoon to make potatoes creamy and well combined.

Adjust seasonings as needed. Add cream and butter if necessary to desired consistency.

Roasted Corn on the Cob with Smokey Chili Butter

Ingredients

4 ears of corn
Salt
Juice of one lime
4 TBSP Smokey Chili Butter

Directions

Heat the grill to high.

Pull the husks of the corn away, but don't remove it. Remove the silk and discard. Sprinkle each ear of corn with salt and pull the husks back down over the ears of corn. Wrap the corn ears in foil and place on the grill. Lower the lid and grill for about 20 minutes turning often to keep from burning and cook evenly.

When the corn is lightly charred and cooked to tender, remove from the heat and clean the husks away. Squeeze the lime juice over the corn and serve with the Smokey Chili Butter.

Roasted Butternut Squash with Citrus Sage Butter

Ingredients

3 cups butternut squash, diced
3/4 cup onion, diced
3 TBSP brown sugar
2 TBSP olive oil
Salt and pepper
4 TBSP Citrus Sage Butter

Directions

Heat oven to 350F.

Coat the squash and onions with the oil and season with the salt and pepper. Spread the vegetables into a large baking dish in one layer. Sprinkle the top with the brown sugar.

Bake for 20 minutes, stirring once. After 20 minutes, stir the squash and dot with the Citrus Sage Butter. Check after 5 minutes and stir the melted butter into the squash. Bake an additional 15 to 20 minutes or until lightly browned and tender.

Pepper and Onion Saute

Ingredients

1 red bell pepper, cut in strips
1 green bell pepper, cut in strips
1 large onion, cut in strips
2 banana peppers, cut in rings
1 jalapeno pepper, diced
3 TBSP Mojito Butter
2 TBSP olive oil
4 green onions, sliced
Juice of one lime

Directions

Heat the olive oil over medium high heat in a large skillet. Add the bell peppers and onion. Saute until vegetables soften.

Add the banana and jalapeno peppers and cook for an additional five minutes.

Add the Mojito butter and green onions. Stir to combine and melt the butter. Saute an additional two to three minutes.

Remove from the heat and drizzle with the lime juice right before serving.

SANDWICHES

CAJUN ROAST BEEF SANDWICH

Ingredients

4 Kaiser rolls, toasted
1 1/2 lbs Cajun style roast beef, sliced for sandwiches
2 large tomatoes, sliced
1 onion, thinly sliced
2 cups baby arugula
4 oz Caper Butter
4 slices provolone cheese
4 Dill pickle spears

Directions

While the bread is still hot from toasting, spread each half liberally with the Caper Butter. Assemble the sandwich with the roast beef, tomato, onion, arugula, and cheese.

Serve with a dill pickle spear.

California Smoked Turkey Sandwich

Ingredients

8 slices whole grain bread, toasted
1 lb smoked turkey, sliced for sandwiches
2 large tomatoes, sliced
1 red onion, thinly sliced
8 slices thick cut bacon
4 slices Swiss cheese
1 cup watercress
4 oz Avocado Lime Butter

Directions

Cook the bacon until crisp. Drain on paper towels. Break each piece in half.

While the bread is still hot from toasting, spread each half liberally with the Avocado Lime Butter. Assemble the sandwich with the turkey, tomatoes, onion, bacon, cheese, and watercress.

Ham and Cheese Sliders

Ingredients

8 slider buns or dinner rolls
1 lb black forest ham, thinly sliced
8 slices Colby-jack cheese
16 dill pickle slices
6 oz Dijon Chive Butter
1 TBSP poppy seeds

Directions

Heat the oven to 350F.

Line a baking dish with foil and spray it with cooking spray.

Slice the rolls in half. Spread each bottom and top liberally with the Dijon Chive Butter on the cut side.

Place the bottoms in the baking dish buttered, cut side up. Cut each slice of cheese in quarters. Place two pieces of the quartered cheese slices on each bottom bun. Place a slice of ham on top of the cheese. Place two dill pickle slices on top of the ham. Add two more pieces of the quartered cheese slices on top of the ham and pickles. Top with the bun tops.

Place a slice of the Dijon Chive Butter on top of each slider. Sprinkle poppy sees over the tops of the sliders.

Cover the baking dish with foil. Bake for 10 to 15 minutes, until the cheese is melted. Remove the foil and cook an additional two to three minutes to lightly brown the tops of the sliders.

HUGE PUB STYLE WHITE CHEDDAR BURGERS

Ingredients

2 lbs ground beef sirloin
Salt and pepper
2 TBSP onion, grated
2 tsp garlic, grated
7 TBSP Honey Worcestershire Butter
1 TBSP vegetable oil
4 thick slices of aged white cheddar (or 8 thin slices)
4 premium large hamburger buns
Country style Dijon mustard
Shredded iceberg lettuce
Dill pickles
Red onion slices
Sliced tomatoes

Directions

Heat the oven to 325F.

Mix the grated onion and garlic with the salt and pepper into the ground beef. Add 2 TBSP of the Honey Worcestershire Butter. Mix until blended, but don't over work the meat. Divide into four sections and make each section into patties.

Heat the vegetable oil in a skillet over medium high heat. Place the hamburger patties into the skillet and brown on the first side for about three minutes. Turn the patties over and brown for an additional two to three minutes.

Place cheese slices on the top of each patty. Place the skillet of hamburger patties into the oven and bake for about five to six minutes for a medium well temperature.

While the patties finish cooking in the oven, butter each side of the buns with the remaining Honey Worcestershire Butter. Heat a second large skillet over medium heat. Place the buns, butter side down, into the hot skillet to melt the butter into the bread and lightly toast.

Take the hamburger patties out of the oven and let rest for about five minutes. Continue preparing the buns if necessary.

Assemble the burgers by adding some Dijon mustard, lettuce, pickles, onion, and tomatoes as desired.

Want to find out when I publish a new book or when I have a sale? Sign up here and you'll always be in the loop!

http://recipesfromeverywhere.com/SignUp

P.S. You'll even get a tasty little bonus!

Recipe Books from Natalie

Special Christmas Recipes - Create a Festive Feast
http://recipesfromeverywhere.com/ChristmasMenus

Elegant Thanksgiving Recipes – Upscale your holiday
http://recipesfromeverywhere.com/ThanksgivingMenus

Christmas Dessert Recipes from Around the World – Sweets to make your holiday merry and bright
http://recipesfromeverywhere.com/Christmas

Romantic Valentine's Day Recipes - Special menus for the one you love
http://recipesfromeverywhere.com/Valentines

St. Patrick's Day Recipes – Celebrating authentic Irish cuisine
http://recipesfromeverywhere.com/StPats

Semi-Traditional Easter Recipes – Savory, sweet, and special
http://recipesfromeverywhere.com/Easter

Mardi Gras Recipes – Party Appetizers and Drinks
http://recipesfromeverywhere.com/mardigras

… Or take a look at my Amazon Page to see everything all in one place
http://recipesfromeverywhere.com/NatalieAtAmazon

One Last Thing

I really hope you enjoyed this book of recipes for flavored butters. I put it together with the hope that you will find yummy ways to punch up your menus with flavor.

If you did enjoy this book, I'd appreciate it if you'd leave a review so that others can use your opinion to help them plan their own meals for delicious food. Here's the link to leave a review:

http://recipesfromeverywhere.com/ButterReview

Thank you!

Notes

Made in the USA
Las Vegas, NV
21 December 2022